SAN LUIS OBISPO

100 YEARS OF DOWNTOWN BUSINESSES

The Cross Streets
OSOS, CHORRO, MORRO, GARDEN, BROAD, NIPOMO STREETS AND MUCH MORE

This book is dedicated to ....

My wonderful wife Janet
&
My daughters
Katie, Kristie, and Kasey
&
My grandchildren Elliott and Scarlett
&
My Mom Sharon and My Dad Bill

SAN LUIS OBISPO

100 YEARS OF DOWNTOWN BUSINESSES

THE CROSS STREETS
OSOS, CHORRO, MORRO, GARDEN, BROAD, NIPOMO STREETS AND MUCH MORE

by
GUY CRABB

Guy Crabb Publishing
San Luis Obispo, California

ISBN-13: 978-0-9790616-7-7

Published by

Guy Crabb Publishing
P.O. Box 994
San Luis Obispo, California 93406

Website: www.slo100years.com
E-Mail: crabbx5@charter.net

Manufactured in the United States of America
Printed by
Thomson-Shore
Dexter, Michigan
USA

Cover Design by
Chiara Ramirez
Short But Sweet Graphics
chiara@shortbutsweet.com

INTRODUCTION

My name is Guy Crabb. I have been an elementary school teacher for 26 years and have a great hobby researching the local history of San Luis Obispo. One of my favorite subjects to teach is social studies. In third grade, the students learn about the history of their local community. In fourth grade, the students learn about California history. Two of my favorite things to teach my students are the history of their community and the history of California. I use items such as adobe bricks, branding irons, a kid's saddle, a lasso, arrowheads, woven baskets, and lots of other things to make the lessons fun and educational. I know I'm teaching a good lesson when I see the wide eyes and open mouths of the kids in the class. I try to make my lessons memorable.

Years ago I was at the Sunset Drive-In swap meet in San Luis Obispo, looking for things to buy for my classroom. I found a man who had a group of old newspapers from the local Tribune newspaper (then the Telegram-Tribune). I knew this would be something cool to share with my class. As I started looking through one of the newspapers, I saw lots of ads. The newspaper was dated 1920. The ads had two-digit phone numbers and most of the ads just had the street that the business was on. Some of the ads had actual addresses and the first thing that went through my head was, "I wonder what's at that address now?" That is how I came up with the idea of writing these books on downtown San Luis Obispo history. I thought that following a certain address for several years would be fun and interesting. It has taken years to gather the research for the books. I have had great opportunities to talk to people from some of the pioneer families of San Luis Obispo. I will name many of these people in the acknowledgement section. My biggest hope for writing these books is that it gives people great memories.

This is my third book on the downtown history of San Luis Obispo. My first book was on Higuera Street and I had a wonderful time writing that book. My second book was the Monterey and Marsh Streets book. This third book and the final book of my trilogy are on the various cross streets of downtown San Luis Obispo. I have continued to use my time line in 5 year increments. There are so many businesses that come and go that you may remember a business that may not show up in the book. My guess is that the business lasted less than 5 years or it was not there on the 5 year mark. I was recently talking with Mike White, the owner of Boo Boo Records on Monterey Street, about how many businesses come and go in our downtown. In my books, there could be a business that was at a location in 1971,1972,1973 and 1974 but not there in 1975, so that business may or may not make it into the book. If I can pinpoint a date with a business change, then I will put that information in my books.

As I write this book in the year 2011, there are many planned changes for downtown San Luis Obispo. I was just downtown the other day and workers were tearing down and doing reconstruction on the old Granada Hotel building on Morro Street. I just happened to be walking around town doing research for this book when I turned right on Morro Street from Higuera and saw the workers on scaffolding working on the old Granada and one of the buildings was completely gone. Wow! I was just down here a few days ago and the old building was still there. I realized and remembered that it only takes a wrecking crew a few hours to tear down a part of history. Today, Tuesday, June 28, 2011, the local newspaper, "The Tribune," did record this historical event in the paper. At least most of the building is still there and the new owners are planning on making it back into a hotel with mixed-use businesses on the ground floor. So this 1920's era building will continue to be enjoyed for at least 100 more years, I hope. The areas in town for future construction include the Chinatown Project, which includes lots of new construction on Palm, Morro, Monterey, and Chorro Streets. On Marsh Street there were big plans to put multi-levels buildings on both Marsh and Garden Streets. After much discussion, the plans were scaled down to size to satisfy many of our citizens, but not all of us.

With all of the research I have conducted over the years, I have seen many changes that San Luis Obispo has gone through. In the early 1930's, our little town tore down several old wooden buildings and put up brick or cement buildings. There used to be a really big building on the corner of Higuera and Garden where Marshall's Jewelry is today, but it was demolished along with several buildings on Monterey Street in the 1970's.

This book will take the reader along many cross streets of downtown San Luis Obispo. We will stroll down Chorro Street and pass by Mission News or Bull's Tavern, which was named after its owner Albert (Bull) Tognazzini. Bull's was previously known as the Budweiser Tavern. There was a time in which it was common to name your bar after the drink that was served frequently to its customers. We will then walk down the historic Osos Street along the J. P. Andrews buildings and look across the street at the old courthouse. We will walk along several other streets in downtown, but that is not all. Back in the 1930's many small Mom and Pop grocery stores popped up around town. I will discuss a little of the history of several of these businesses.

Even though this is the last street book of downtown, I hope to continue to update them every 10 years or so. I do encourage everyone to go visit downtown and start enjoying what it is today, because it will change. Take pictures of you and your family in front of some of these buildings. In 20 or 30 years you will be happy you took those few moments to snap that photo. It's great to remember the past and enjoy the future.

ACKNOWLEDGMENTS

My first acknowledgement goes to my wonderful wife Janet Crabb. She has continued to support me throughout this wonderfully crazy project. She is my best supporter, editor, and my computer expert and of course my best friend. My next acknowledgement goes to the San Luis Obispo History Center. The research center at the Museum has provided me with a remarkable assortment of photos and facts on the cross streets of downtown San Luis Obispo. I would also like to thank the ladies at the San Luis Obispo City Library in the special collections room. Writing a book like this has taken years of research and I have used many local historical books as references. The following publications have helped me with my research: "Telegram Tribune" from 1905 – 2011; Polk directories; Pioneers of San Luis Obispo County and Environs, by Annie Morrison and John H. Haydon; San Luis Obispo Discoveries, by Paul Tritenbach; Parade Along the Creek, by Rose McKeen; "La Vista", a periodical published by the San Luis Obispo Historical Society in the 1980's; many Cal Poly yearbooks; Discovering San Luis Obispo County, by Carleton Winslow; Old Times, by Charles A. Maino, and a great collection of pictures and other artifacts from Wendell Wheeler.

There are several people who have been nice enough to talk to me about the history of downtown businesses. I would like to thank these individuals: Charles Kamm, Jack Feliciano, Dean Miller, Steve Owens, Ted Wheeler, David Middlecamp, who has a wonderful blog on the history of SLO called Photos from the Vault www.sloblogs.thetribunenews.com/slovault/, Jim Hill, Jean Martin, and Matt Moore. I have also had the opportunity to talk to business owners, construction workers, joggers, barbers, visitors, long-time residents, and many other people during the writing of this book. I can say that walking around talking with the people of San Luis Obispo makes me realize that I live in one of the nicest places in the world.

All of the current photos in the book were taken by me in the early morning to avoid the cars that park along the streets. A few people in the above acknowledgements also allowed me to use a photograph from their collections. Many of the postcards and photos that I have used were bought from people across the country through the use of the internet.

Finally, I would like to acknowledge my family for supporting me and encouraging my efforts in writing these three books. My wife Janet and my three daughters Kasey, Kristie, and Katie are four important people in my life who have given me encouragement to keep writing and fulfilling a passion of sharing the history of SLO.

TABLE OF CONTENTS

Please enjoy your memories!

Chorro Street

940
Chorro

940 Chorro Street

- ➢ 2005 – 2011   Red Hot Pottery
- ➢ 1995 – 2000   Nectar of Bean
- ➢ 1990   Stitcher Tailoring
- ➢ 1960 – 1985   State Board of Equalization
- ➢ 1945   Carpenters Local Union

942
Chorro

942 Chorro Street

- ➤ 2011   vacant
- ➤ 2005 – 2010   Wells Fargo Financial
- ➤ 1995 – 2000   Northwest Financial
- ➤ 1980 – 1990   Norwood Bookshop
- ➤ 1970 – 1975   Kuan Yin Book Store
- ➤ 1960 – 1965   Accounting Business (Boyce)

**950
Chorro**

950 Chorro Street

➤ 2011   Sweet Earth Chocolates as of
                    June 2011
➤ 2009 - 2011   Ja Nene
➤ 2005 – 2009   Letter Bank
➤ 2000   Clever Li Li Clothing
➤ 1990 – 1995   Clothing store
➤ 1980 – 1985   Backdoor gifts
➤ 1969 – 1975   **Persian Market gifts**
➤ 1965   McLain Photography
➤ 1955 – 1960   Stauch Painting Contractor

952
Chorro

952 Chorro Street

- ➢ 2010   Trio Boutique and partly in 950 Chorro
- ➢ 2005 -2010   Yellow Kiss
- ➢ 2000   ?
- ➢ 1995   Vacant
- ➢ 1990   Johnson Art and Framing
- ➢ 1985   Vacant
- ➢ 1980   Calico n Canvas
- ➢ 1970 – 1975   State Department of Employment

956
Chorro

956 Chorro Street

- ➤ 2005 - 2011   Growing Grounds
- ➤ 2005   Art and Sol art gallery
- ➤ 2000   Plants and Gifts
- ➤ 1990 – 1995   Secret Garden
- ➤ 1960 – 1985   I could find no business during this time

At one time during the 1800's this property was used
as the kitchen for the adobe next door.

964 Chorro Street

The Sauer (pronounced Sour) Adobe has a very long and varied history. It seems many people have stories that have some similarities and differences. It's always hard to figure out who has the correct story. I will give you a little history using a combination of these various stories. The Sauer Adobe was once a single story adobe that was probably part of the mission complex. It was built in the early 1800's out of mud and straw abode bricks. In 1860 a German newcomer, George Sauer (or possibly Frederick Sauer), bought the property and added a second story to his new home. To add to the romance of the building, there seems to be a ghost that haunts the upstairs. In 1940, Helen Adams bought the property and operated a tearoom and boarding house. Mrs. Adams is credited for restoring the adobe during the early 1960's. Today the adobe is known as the Sauer-Adams Adobe.

Year 1969

964
Chorro

964 Chorro Street, Sauer Adobe

➤ 1955 – 2011   Multiple businesses. Some of the businesses over the years were: Real Estate businesses, San Luis Employment, Answering Service, saloon, boarding house, apartments, restaurants, hotels, and many more types of businesses. This was a personal home to several families over the years. In 2011 Adobe Realty, Heaven and Earth ,and Yarns at the Adobe occupy 964 Chorro

➤ 1950   San Luis Employment Agency
➤ 1940   Italian restaurant
➤ 1930   Swiss American Hotel

In 1887 the San Luis Obispo Board of Trade announced that they had spent $2,684 for the promotion of the city and the county. They published 25,000 brochures and 25,000 copies of a booklet featuring the city. Since those days the Board of Trade has been replaced by the Chamber of Commerce which has continued to promote the city. The groovy brochure to the right was published by the San Luis Obispo Chamber of Commerce when it was located on Marsh Street during the 1960's. Inside, the brochure tells the reader places to stay, places to eat and services to use as well as places to see.

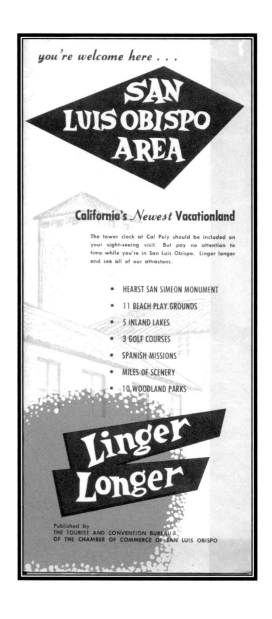

you're welcome here . . .

SAN
LUIS OBISPO
AREA

California's *Newest* Vacationland

The tower clock at Cal Poly should be included on your sight-seeing visit. But pay no attention to time while you're in San Luis Obispo. Linger longer and see all of our attractions.

- HEARST SAN SIMEON MONUMENT
- 11 BEACH PLAY GROUNDS
- 5 INLAND LAKES
- 3 GOLF COURSES
- SPANISH MISSIONS
- MILES OF SCENERY
- 10 WOODLAND PARKS

Linger
Longer

Published by
THE TOURIST AND CONVENTION BUREAU
OF THE CHAMBER OF COMMERCE OF SAN LUIS OBISPO

970
Chorro

970 Chorro Street

- ➤ 2005 – 2011   Bliss Body Spa
- ➤ 2000   Body Spa
- ➤ 1995   Scandinavian Body
- ➤ 1990   Sun Employment
- ➤ 1985   Gold Concept jewelry
- ➤ 1970 – 1980   **Courtyard gifts**
- ➤ 1965   San Luis Obispo Art Gallery
- ➤ 1950 – 1960   **McLain Photography**
- ➤ 1860   Sauer Grocery and Bakery

Chorro Street and Monterey Street, circa 1930's

This is a classic picture of a rider and his horse. The part of the picture
that interests me the most is the view down Monterey Street to see the old
Blackstone Hotel. The building on the left was a two story wooden structure
and the mission is next to the two story structure. The rider was probably
preparing for a parade or other special celebration.

984
Chorro

984 Chorro Street

- ➢ 2008 – 2011   Vacant due to redevelopment plans
- ➢ 1985 - 2008   Costume Capers closed Aug. 15 2008
- ➢ 1985   Choice clothing's
- ➢ 1980   Vacant
- ➢ 1975   Circa Seventy-Four gifts
- ➢ 1970   K-T Bible

Mission Plaza
Chorro

Mission San Luis Obispo is the heart of San Luis Obispo, and the area in front of the mission has been a gathering place since the mission began construction in 1772. Today we call the area in front of the mission "Mission Plaza." The area in front of the mission was once a very busy Monterey Street which was lined with businesses since the early 1800's. By November, 1970, the first phase of the Mission Plaza as we know it today was completed. Monterey Street was closed and the plaza became a popular pedestrian walkway and a gathering place for the city.

Chorro Street and Monterey Street, circa late 1800's

This is a seldom seen picture of the Laser Building on the left and the mission in the middle, with an old two story framed business building on the right. The framed building was once a thriving business location with many different businesses, such as a gun shop and saloon with rooms for rent above. This poor building had its problems over the years with cars and trucks smashing into it as they came driving down Monterey Street from the Cuesta Grade. After many years of neglect, the two-story framed building was demolished around 1955. Today the bear fountain is in the area of the old framed building along with mission gardens and trees. Mission San Luis Obispo has an interesting distinction: it doesn't have a cemetery like most missions. The cemetery would normally have been located where this framed structure was or very near the church building.

Laser Building, Chorro Street

These are two pictures of the once famous Laser Building which was built circa 1880. This building was on the corner of Chorro and Monterey Streets and housed a variety of businesses including Tribune Printing, a brewery, French Hotel, taxi service, transportation depot, a garage, barber shop, butcher shop, and more. The story of its demise is varied. Some stories say it was demolished due to unsafe conditions and another story has an out of control truck barreling down Monterey Street after losing its brakes coming down Cuesta Grade and smashing into the corner of the building. According to this story, due to the damage the building was declared unsafe and had to be demolished. These pictures are part of the Historical Museum collection.

1023 Chorro

1023 Chorro Street

- ➤ 2011   Cielo Cantina
- ➤ 2010 - 2011   Native Lounge
- ➤ 2005   Mission Grill
- ➤ 2000   Vacant
- ➤ 1996   Mongo's
- ➤ 1975 – 1990   Sebastian's Restaurant
- ➤ 1930 – 1970   **Berkemeyer Market**
- ➤ 1925   Vacant or old building was demolished
- ➤ 1910 – 1920   Cigar/Saloon (Stearns)
- ➤ 1905   Saloon (Mchlmenn)

Chorro Street, circa 1930's

Chorro Street has a very interesting history. Chorro Street was the main road into San Luis Obispo if you were coming from Chorro Valley (the valley between Morro Bay and San Luis Obispo), Morro Bay or any other place on the north coast. In the 1870's, Chorro was not the wonderful link between Monterey and Higuera Streets that it is today. During this time Chorro Street ended at Monterey Street because the creek ran freely through town between the two streets. The area between the two major streets was nothing more than a field which soon became full of buildings and businesses occupying the area that would be now be considered the center of Chorro Street. The citizens of the city decided that Chorro Street needed to connect to Higuera and the city went into negotiations with the property owner. The land owner was aware how much the city wanted his property, so negotiations became strained. A deal was finally struck, buildings removed, the street widened, and in 1874 a wooden bridge was built across the creek which became a major improvement for transportation in the city.

Name That Building

Here's a fun game. Can you name where the building is for each of the pictures below?

Picture A

Picture C

Picture B

Picture D

1026 Chorro Street, Wickenden/Wade Building

1026 Chorro is the address for businesses on the second floor of the Wickenden building, which was built around 1909. The Wickenden family occupied the ground floor of this building with their clothing store from 1912 to the late 1960's. This building has also been called the Wade Building because an obstetrician named Dr. Lyman T. Wade had offices on the second floor from 1915 to the late 1930's. Over the years there have been a wide variety of businesses that have occupied the second floor of this beautiful building.

This picture was taken before the 2010-2011 retrofit. Most of businesses are now gone and **Bull's** is at 1040 but for historical sake the addresses below were in use for years.

1028-1030-1032
1036-1036.5
Chorro

1028 – 1030 – 1032 – 1036 – 1036.5 Chorro Street

Address 1028
- ➢ 2000 – 2010 — SLO Perks
- ➢ 1995 — Nancy Anne Coffee
- ➢ 1983 – 1990 — Michael Optical
- ➢ 1975 – 1980 — Buslong Realty
- ➢ 1950 – 1970 — Unknown
- ➢ 1940 – 1945 — Arrowhead Distributor
- ➢ 1935 — Chamber of Commerce
- ➢ 1910 – 1930 — Insurance and Real Estate

Address 1030
- ➢ 1905 – 2010 — Mission News

Address 1032
- ➢ 1955 – 2010 — Bull's Tarven
- ➢ 1940 – 1950 — Budweiser Tarven
- ➢ 1930 — Art Goods (Gingg)
- ➢ 1915 — Crockery
- ➢ 1905 – 1910 — San Luis Produce Market

Address 1036
- ➢ 2005 – 1980 — Yervant Jewelry
- ➢ 1975 — Jeanine's Jewelry
- ➢ 1970 — Merle Cosmetics
- ➢ 1965 — Alberts Jewelry
- ➢ 1945 – 1960 — Camera Shop
- ➢ 1940 — Art Supplies
- ➢ 1930 – 1935 — Beauty Shop (Rockwell)

Address 1036.5
- ➢ 1995 – 2005 — Stamp San Luis
- ➢ 1990 — Coastal Travel
- ➢ 1980 – 85 — Animal Crackers Maternity
- ➢ 1970 – 1975 — Billie Maternity Shop
- ➢ 1965 — Magic Fashion
- ➢ 1960 — Shoe Repair

This building is under retrofitting during 2009-2010

Bull's Tavern / Chorro Street

Bull's Tavern has had a rich and colorful history. During the 1930's and 1940's many bars were named after their main beer distributor. Budweiser was a very popular beer and **Budweiser Taverns** started popping up all over the country. The name of our local tavern changed after the proprietor of the bar, Albert (Bull) Tognazzini, renamed the bar **Bull's** after himself.

1029
Chorro

1029 Chorro Street

➤ 2010 – 2011   Infin8 Beauty
➤ 2000 – 2009   SLO Swim
➤ 1990 – 1995   Optometrist (Coombs)
➤ 1980 – 1985   Optometrist (Chaffee)
➤ 1955 – 1975   Optometrist (Williams)
➤ 1945 – 1950   Optometrist (Petersen)
➤ 1935 – 1940   Optometrist (Hamblen)

Your Headquarters for . . . .
WRANGLERS PANTS and SHIRTS

BURRISS SADDLERY

HYER, JUSTIN, ACME, and TEXAS BOOTS
RIDING EQUIPMENT
SAMSONITE LUGGAGE

*

W. E. BURRISS, Manager

*

Phone 543-4101

1033 Chorro Street   San Luis Obispo, California

1033 Chorro Street

- ➤ 2010 – 2011   San Luis Riders/ Hep Kat clothing as of July 2011
- ➤ 2000 – 2005   Unique Beads
- ➤ 1955 – 1995   **Burriss Saddery**
- ➤ 1945 – 1950   Forden's Hardware
- ➤ 1940   Hardware store
- ➤ 1905 – 1910   Wickenden's Grocery

This is the Dughi Building, which was constructed in 1885. Paul Dughi was born in Switzerland in the 1850's and traveled to San Luis Obispo in the 1870's. He was a dairy foreman and businessman in town. He married Mary Villa and they had 9 children together.

1035 Chorro Street

- ➢ 2011   Bliss Café as of July 2011
- ➢ 1985 – 2009   **Cowboy Cookie**
- ➢ 1975 – 1980   Franklin Electric House Restaurant
- ➢ 1970   Exquisite Wigs
- ➢ 1945 – 1965   Insurance/Real Estate
- ➢ 1940   Merl's Candy
- ➢ 1935   Wooden Shoe Café
- ➢ 1920 – 1930   St. Clair News Agency
- ➢ 1910 – 1915   Candy Store (St. Clair)
- ➢ 1905   Candy Store (Dunning)

1037
Chorro

1037 Chorro Street

- ➢ 2010 – 2011   Pithy Little Wine Co./
                     Minerva clothing as of July2011
- ➢ 2000 – 2005   **Bali Isle**
- ➢ 1995   Unique Beads
- ➢ 1990   Made in SLO gifts
- ➢ 1975 – 1985   Bookhaven
- ➢ 1970   Del Sur gift shop
- ➢ 1955 – 1965   Helen's Millinery
- ➢ 1945   Beauty Shop (Gratton)
- ➢ 1935 – 1940   Clarence Brown Jewelry
- ➢ 1930   Stage Lines/Hill's Sporting Goods
- ➢ 1910   Saloon (Hardison)

1039
Chorro

Chamber of Commerce

- ➤ 1970 – 2011   Chamber of Commerce
- ➤ 1960 – 1965   Stronis Gun and Sports
- ➤ 1940 – 1955   Hill's Sporting Goods
- ➤ 1910 – 1915   San Luis Building and Loan
- ➤ 1905   Insurance Office

Changes
On
Chorro

The Wickenden Building (or the Wade Building—you can pick), at 1026 Chorro, has long been an important business location in town. The building has been going through its retrofitting construction from 2010 into 2011. **Bull's** has been moved

down the block to 1040 Chorro, which revives an old address used by the **Palace Barber Shop** from 1905 – 1955. The rest of the building is now occupied by **Nautical Bean** and **SLO Pastry Co**.

CALIFORNIA'S FINEST CENTRAL COAST STORE
SINCE 1887

featuring famous brand names
...with a fine reputation

SINCE 1887
RILEYS
CENTRAL CALIFORNIA

SHOP ALL THREE STORES
Rileys Downtown
—Chorro at Marsh
Rileys College Square
—College Square
Rileys Home Furnishings
—College Square

After the 2010-2011 Wineman Hotel retrofit, new businesses will once again occupy the even-address side of the block.

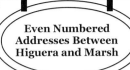

Even Numbered Addresses Between Higuera and Marsh

The building on the right side of the street as you look at the picture has even-numbered businesses on Chorro Street between Higuera and Monterey Streets.

- ➢ 1935 – 1960   Wineman Barber
- ➢ 1975 – 2000   **Riley's Department Store**
- ➢ 1945 – 1970   Smart Shoppee
- ➢ 1940   Cornelia's gift shop
- ➢ 1935   Ru-Mae Shoppee
- ➢ 1955 – 1960   Schroeder's Studio of Photo
- ➢ 1940   Powder Puff Beauty Shop
- ➢ 1935   Dr. Butler
- ➢ 1935 – 1960   Evans Brokerage
- ➢ 1910 – 1920   Tribune Printing Co.

Past Businesses On Chorro

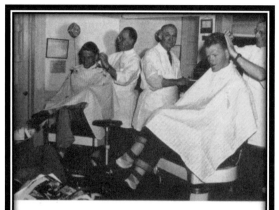

Three chairs and three barbers reign supreme at the Palace, assuring a minimum of waiting by their subjects. On throne number three we see student Fred Broemmer being prepared to look like a prince by Earl L. Parker. On throne number two Ben Broerma is being groomed by Master Barber Bob Baldridge. "King" Earl Twitchell mans the cash drawer enroute from throne number one. You are always treated royally at the Palace!

Palace Barber Shop
1038 CHORRO

THE CAMERA SHOP

Photo Finishing — Photo Supplies

1036 Chorro　　　　　　　　　**Phone 1748**

Real estate and insurance is handled by the best informed source in San Luis Obispo. Evans Brokerage Co. is always ready to give expert advice. H. R. Baruther has the bull by the horns while Cecil Evans and George Ross point to their respective names and specialized line on the window of their headquarters at 1118 Chorro St. Seated at the desk are Gerald B. Evans, insurance specialist, and the office secretary, Mrs. Jack C. Bolton, Cal Poly student wife.

Evans Brokerage Co.
1118 CHORRO ST.

Page Two Hundred Sixty-one

1111 Chorro Street

- ➤ 1995 – 2011   Sancturary Tabacco
- ➤ 1975 – 1990   Puff N' Stuff Tabacco
- ➤ 1965 – 1970   **Mission Realty**
- ➤ 1960   Vacant
- ➤ 1955   Prudential Insurance
- ➤ 1920   West Coast Land
- ➤ 1915   Real Estate

1117 Chorro Street

- ➤ 2000 – 2011   Black Sheep
- ➤ 1990 – 1995   Nothing But The Best
- ➤ 1985   LeCroissent Restaurant
- ➤ 1975 – 1980   Real Estate (Matulich)
- ➤ 1950 – 1970   Minelle's Lingerie
- ➤ 1940 – 1945   Wee Shop
- ➤ 1935   Cigar Shop
- ➤ 1920   Optometrist (Gowan)
- ➤ 1905 – 1910   Sunset Telephone and Telegraph

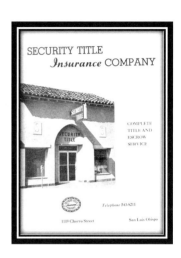

1119 Chorro Street

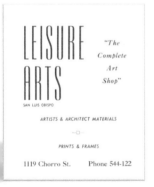

- 2010 - 2011   Atmosphere Furnishing/Vacant early 2011
- 2005   Temporary business/less than a year
- 1995 – 2000   Games People Play
- 1990   Mary Ann's Hallmark
- 1980 – 1985   Hill's Hallmark
- 1970   **Leisure Arts**
- 1930 – 1965   **Security Title Insurance**
- 1920   Loomis and Sons (grain buyers)
- 1905   Doctor office (Sinclair)

1121-1123-1127-1131 Chorro

This building has been a single business and has also been divided into multiple businesses over the years. Below are some of the businesses and addresses that have occupied this section of Chorro Street over the past 100 years.

1121 – 1123 – 1127 - 1131 Chorro Street

- ➤ 1940 – 1945   Beauty Art Salon
- ➤ 1930 – 1935   Accountant (Boyce)
- ➤ 1945 – 1950   Ru-Mae Shoppee
- ➤ 2010 – 2011   Fed Ex
- ➤ 1995 – 2000   Mary Ann's Hallmark
- ➤ 1980 – 1990   Hill's Office Products
- ➤ 1945 – 1975   Hill's Stationary Store
- ➤ 1945 – 1950   Irene's Beauty Shop
- ➤ 1970 – 1980   Nutrition
- ➤ 1945 – 1950   Hill's Offset
- ➤ 1920 – 1930   Santa Maria Gas Co.
- ➤ 1905   EE Long Piano (1131-1133)

Here's the answers to the Name That Building on page 17:

- The Cat is a square of the Children's Museum on Nipomo Street.
- The 1987 brick sign is on the city library building on Palm Street.
- The rock wall is on the old city library which is now known as SLO Little Theater on Morro Street.
- The scary sea monsters are on the City Hall building on Palm Street.

How many did you get correct?

More San Luis Obispo trivia:

1. Madonna Road was once named French Road.
2. There was once a Piggly Wiggly store in SLO.
3. McLintock's was once a Spud-Nut donut store.
4. The first French Hospital was on Marsh.
5. The end of Marsh Street was once an actual marsh.
6. The second floor of the Warden Building is very cool.
7. Some people say a building on Morro Street once had a speak-easy in the basement.
8. There is a restaurant downtown that was once the coroner's office.
9. An article in the *American City* magazine in 1918 wrote about the new city lighting system along the downtown streets of San Luis Obispo.

1135 Chorro

1135 Chorro Street

- ➤ 1990 – 2011   San Luis Luggage
- ➤ 1975 – 1985   Owen's Music
- ➤ 1970   Carriage House Gallery
- ➤ 1965   Title Insurance
- ➤ 1960   Water Colors Art Materials
- ➤ 1950   Tax Consultant
- ➤ 1945   Internal Revenue Service
- ➤ 1935 – 1940   San Luis Building and Loan

1141
Chorro

1141 Chorro Street

- ➤ 2011   Vacant/Eureka Burger July 2011
- ➤ 2005 – 2010   Corner View Restaurant
- ➤ 1995 – 2000   Linn's Restaurant
- ➤ 1990   Home Federal
- ➤ 1980 – 1985   Mission Federal Saving and Loan
- ➤ 1960 – 1975   **Title Insurance**
- ➤ 1955   South Counties Gas Co.
- ➤ 1935 – 1945   Santa Maria Gas Co.

1235
Chorro

1235 Chorro Street

- ➤ 2010 – 2011   Chase Bank
- ➤ 2000 – 2010   Washington Mutual
- ➤ 1975 – 1995   Great Western Savings
- ➤ 1970   **Central Savings**
- ➤ 1960 – 1965   Saving and Loan

Osos Street

Osos Street

Osos Street is as historical as any other street in San Luis Obispo. The name Osos means "bear," which were abundant when the first Spaniards arrived in our city. The citizens chose to name Osos Street in honor of the animal and the valley that was also called Canada de Los Osos or Valley of the Bears. The above picture shows the J.P. Andrews extension buildings that he built along Osos Street. Mr. Andrews decided to build a modern classic brick building which replaced the wooden hotel that once stood at this site. The corner of Osos and Monterey Streets was once a main intersection in town, and continues to be a major intersection and tourist attraction in the city.

Hotel Andrews Osos Street, circa 1920's

The old Hotel Andrews was built in 1910 at the corner of Osos and Palm Streets. It was demolished in 1966 and the new city library was built in 1989 at the site. The Hotel Andrews was a wonderful hotel that had modern rooms for the time period and one of the town's best restaurants. The hotel was also known for one of the most famous murders in San Luis Obispo. Here's the gruesome story. In July of 1947, a trunk was discovered behind the Hotel Andrews under some stairs by the kitchen delivery door. An employee was puzzled about the trunk and went to open it up. To her horror, inside was the dead body of a woman. It was soon learned that the body was that of Helen King, a one time Countess from Portugal. She was married to Morley King who had disappeared until he was tracked down by the FBI. The murder was in the local newspapers as well as newspapers from Los Angles to San Francisco.

967 Osos Street

- ➤ 2000 – 2011   Wushu and Taichi Center
- ➤ 1995   Environment Center
- ➤ 1985 – 1989   Rainbow Theater
- ➤ 1980   Cinema Zoo
- ➤ 1975   Morro Club Restaurant
- ➤ 1970   Cattleman's Restaurant
- ➤ 1960 – 1965   County offices
- ➤ 1945 – 1955   County Commission offices
- ➤ 1930 - 1935   San Luis Obispo Library
- ➤ 1920   **Hammond Auto Sales**
- ➤ 1910   Novelty Theater

971 Osos

The building is largely unchanged today from this 1930's photo.

971 Osos Street

- ➤ 2000 – 2011   Architects (Fraser)
- ➤ 1965   Cattleman's Restaurant
- ➤ 1960   County offices
- ➤ 1955   The Reporter newspaper
- ➤ 1945   Golden West newspaper
- ➤ 1935   SLO County Superintendent office
- ➤ 1915 – 1920   Telegram
- ➤ 1905 – 1910   Daily Telegram/Printer

975
Osos

975 Osos Street

- ➤ 2010 – 2011   Coastal Communities Physician Network
- ➤ 2000 – 2005   Architects / Insurance
- ➤ 1995   Adobe Travel
- ➤ 1990   Don Pablos Mexican Restaurant
- ➤ 1985   Los Hermano's Restaurant
- ➤ 1975   San Luis Noodle Co.
- ➤ 1970   New Tavern
- ➤ 1965   Irishman Tavern
- ➤ 1930 – 1960   Waldorf Café/Cigar/Tavern
- ➤ 1910 – 1915   Daily Telegram / Printer
- ➤ 1905   Andrews Rooming House

**979
Osos**

979 Osos Street   Upstairs

- ➤ 1980 – 2011   Multiple businesses
- ➤ 1975   Vacant
- ➤ 1955 – 1970   Fremont Hotel
- ➤ 1950   Hotel (Brovelli)
- ➤ 1925 – 1945   Plaza Hotel
- ➤ 1915 – 1920   Court Hotel
- ➤ 1910   Furnished rooms

County
Court House
Osos

Osos Street County Courthouse, circa 1970's

The "old" courthouse was brand new when it was finally completed in 1941. During the late 1930's, the county joined forces with the Works Progress Administration (WPA) and the State Relief Administration (SRA) to build the courthouse. The "really old" courthouse was actually torn down by a very young Alex Madonna when he was around 19 years old. There are wonderful steps that a person walks up to enter the old courthouse. Today these steps are seldom used due to the construction of a new courthouse on Palm Street. The above picture is probably from around the 1970's because the person who took the picture was standing in an empty parking lot across from the courthouse, which is where the city library stands today.

981-983 Osos

981 - 983 Osos Street

Address 981
- 2010-2011   Anderson and Bettencourt Attorney
- 2000 – 2005   Vizdom Software
- 1995   Cal West Productions
- 1990   Real Estate
- 1980 – 1985   Attorney (Shaw)
- 1975   Attorney
- 1965 – 1970   Salvation Army
- 1945 – 1960   Preuss Press
- 1930 – 1935   Printers
- 1915   Vulccanizer (tires)

Address 983
- 2010 – 2011   Lisa Wise Consulting
- 2005   Resource Capitalist
- 2000   Art Development
- 1995   Court Reporting (Wiley)
- 1990   Architect
- 1980 – 1985   Don Patrick Realty
- 1975   Willett Realty
- 1965 – 1970   Vacant
- 1960   Preuss Press
- 1945 – 1950   Perfect Method Cleaners
- 1930   Railway Express Agency
- 1915   Wells Fargo Express
- 1910   Express Agency

987 - 991
Osos

987 – 991 Osos Street

Address 987
- ➤ 2010 – 2011   Weatherford & West Esq.
- ➤ 2000 – 2005   Attorney
- ➤ 1985 – 1995   Architect
- ➤ 1975 – 1980   Hittenberger's Limbs
- ➤ 1970   vacant
- ➤ 1960 – 1965   Paul's Dry Cleaners
- ➤ 1950 – 1955   Rice Travel/ Credit Bureau
- ➤ 1945   Rice Travel/ Chamber of Commerce
- ➤ 1935   County Purchasing
- ➤ 1910 – 1915   Insurance offices
- ➤ 1905   Millinery

Address 991
- ➤ 2010 - 2011   Maguire & Ashbaugh Esq.
- ➤ 1985 – 2005   Attorney
- ➤ 1970 – 1980   Architects
- ➤ 1965   Vacant
- ➤ 1955 – 1960   Attorney (Shipsey & Seitz)
- ➤ 1950   American Red Cross

These are some of the businesses that were once on the corner of Osos and Monterey Streets:

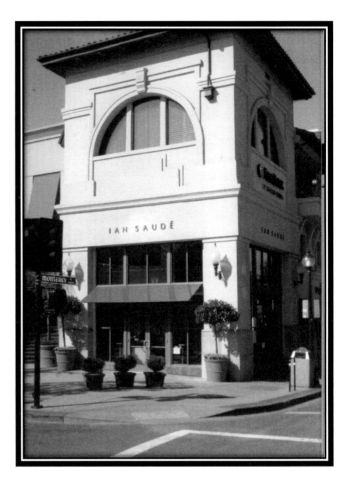

- 1975   Osos Street Records
- 1975   Sal's Shine Shoes
- 1970   Leather goods
- 1965   Lusitana Travel
- 1960   Barber Shop
- 1945 – 1950   Jewelry
- 1920   Central Garage
- 1905 – 1915   Livery stables

This is the corner of Osos and Monterey Streets. There were several businesses along this side of Osos Street down to Higuera. At the turn of the century this whole block was the city livery stables. As time rolled on, the livery stables turned into automotive garages and then turned into smaller businesses and then turned into a parking lot. Once this corner was part of the Obispo Theater building as well. Actually this was one of my favorite parking lots because it was in such a convenient location to the center of downtown. Since time does not stand still, my favorite parking lot turned into a large shopping complex that has many very popular stores.

December 28, 1975, Obispo Theater

This is an action photo of the day the Obispo Theater burned down December 28, 1975. The theater was part of a building that was on the corner of Osos and Monterey Streets. The building was constructed in 1911 when it was originally called El Monterey Theater. In 1928, W.P. Martin bought the theater and renamed it the Obispo Theater. Back in those days the theater had a large pipe organ which was used during the silent movie era and later played for the entertainment of the theater crowd. As you can see on the marquee, Snow White and the Seven Dwarfs was the last movie to be played at the theater on that day in 1975.

**1050
Osos**

1050 Osos Street

1050 Osos Street was the
addresses for several different
government offices over the years.
Then in 1992, 1050 became a fitness
club. This address became Kennedy
Fitness Center in 1992, and when they
vacated the building in 2007, several
different fitness clubs came in to fill
the void for a downtown fitness center.

The next address down the block
is 1060. You need to walk down into
this business, but unfortunately this
address has not been able to keep a
business thriving for more than a few
years at a time. I always thought this
was a really cool business site and one
of these days the right business will
come in and be successful.

Morro Street

888
Morro

888 Morro Street

➤ 2011 – 1995   San Luis Obispo Little Theater
➤ 1955 – 1995   San Luis Obispo City Library

Morro Street is one of the original streets in downtown San Luis Obispo. A map from 1870 shows Morro Street only being 5 blocks long, and the spelling is "Moro." More than likely, Morro Street was named due to the street being pointed in the direction of the town of Morro Bay.

955 Morro

955 Morro Street

- ➤ 2011 – 1990   Public Works offices/Vacant 2011
- ➤ 1985   Vacant
- ➤ 1980   Premier Music Co.
- ➤ 1975   San Luis British Motors
- ➤ 1965 – 1970   Lucksinger Motors
- ➤ 1960   Morganti Liquor

Steve's Taxi PHONE 10-J
NEXT TO OBISPO THEATER
DAY AND NIGHT SERVICE
1016 MORRO ST.   SAN LUIS OBISPO, CAL.

1016 Morro

1016 Morro Street

- 1986 – 2011   Mannikins Tailoring
- 1980   Mauricio Tailoring
- 1970 – 1975   Kiel's Tailoring
- 1960 – 1965   Gus Tailoring
- 1955   San Luis Garbage
- 1935 – 1945   **Steve's Taxi**

1009 Morro

1009 Morro Street, Paiarola Building

➢ 2011 – 1960   Multiple businesses
➢ 1955   Employment office/Tax office
➢ 1940 – 1945   San Luis Obispo City Health

The picture at the top of the page is the original Paiarola Building. The picture was taken in the early 1900's.

1019 Morro Street

- ➢ 1990 – 2011   Dance Shop
- ➢ 1975 – 1985   Mi Lisa's
- ➢ 1950 – 1970   **Beno's Department Store**
- ➢ 1935 – 1945   Tailor
- ➢ 1925   Chiropractor

1021 Morro

1021 Morro Street

- ➤ 2000 – 2011   Kloz
- ➤ 1995   Paper Reeds
- ➤ 1960 – 1990   United Barbers
- ➤ 1930 – 1935   Chiropracter

Gino's Italian Kitchen

"Watch the two chefs prepare the finest Italian food" and try Gino's Pizza!

1023 Morro   Phone 1170

INTER-STATE PRESS-LOS ANGELES
MADE IN U.S.A.

FLAG OF AMERICA

IF WE PLEASE YOU
TELL OTHERS
IF WE DON'T—TELL US

DON'S COFFEE POT CAFE
1015 Morro Street
San Luis Obispo
Open 24 Hours
Every Day
Except Wednesday

BENO'S

Store for Men and Boys

"Everything from suits to shoestrings"

1019 Morro   Phone 620

Special Sunday Dinner
Lunch 50c
Table D'Hote Dinners
A La Carte Service
Club Breakfasts

1020 MORRO ST.

PAUL
PERROT'S GRILL
San Luis Obispo, Calif.

French Cusine
Bar and Cocktail Lounge
Dancing Every
Evening

SAN LUIS OBISPO, CAL.

1023 Morro

1023 Morro Street

- ➤ 2010 – 2011   Bella's
- ➤ 2000 – 2005   Joann's
- ➤ 1990 – 1995   Strauss Luggage
- ➤ 1980 – 1985   Dance Shop
- ➤ 1965 – 1975   Fyr-Fyter Equip.
- ➤ 1960   Grangers Federal Credit
- ➤ 1945   Ten-Twenty-Three Club
- ➤ 1940   Pete's Place
- ➤ 1935   Cigars

A great story that I have heard several times for this single block of Morro Street between Monterey and Higuera Streets, was that there were one or two "speak easys" in the basements of a few addresses along this block. The penalty for being caught with liquor was often a $100 fine and a warning not to do it again. Prohibition lasted from 1920 – 1933. Avila Beach was a popular area where rum was delivered from boats in the dead of the night and the rum runners brought the liquor to the speak easys in the county.

San Luis Obispo County's Only Complete
CHILDREN'S SHOE STORE
We will be Open Sunday, March 27th 11:00-4:00
for your Shopping Convenience

- Buster Brown • Nike
- Jordache • Keds
- Little Capezios
- Bass • Wild Cats
- Kid Power
- Minnetonka Mocs

TOLLEY'S Buster Brown Shoes

Join Our 13 Pair Club

1022 Morro St.

30 Years Experience   San Luis Obispo   541-5020

1022 Morro Street

➤ 2011 – 2005   Aprapos
➤ 2000   Flowers in the Attic
➤ 1982- 1990   **Tolley's Buster Brown Shoes**
➤ 1975 – 1980   Friar Tucks Refectory
➤ 1945   Nisbet's
➤ 1940   Boneiti Travel

1024-1026-1030-1034 Morro Street

During the 1940's and 1950's, this side of the block of Morro Street was very busy. There were four different addresses after the Anderson Hotel building section along the block:

➢ 1024 Morro was home to Country Kitchen in 1960-65 as well as a Soft Drink Parlor in 1930.
➢ 1026 Morro was home to a barber shop for over 10 years and was a liquor store in 1940.
➢ 1030 Morro was home to American Shoe Shine in 1940 and Gus and Gus Cleaners in 1945.
➢ 1034 Morro was home to Robascotti Café from around 1940's into the 1950's.

In the 1970's there was some major construction to the building, and from that point on the building was constructed to have just one business. This great picture from the County Historical Center archives shows the GallenKamp's Shoe Store, which was on the corner of Morro and Higuera Streets in the 1950's and 1960's.

1116-1118
Morro

1116-1118 Morro Street

Address 1116
- ➤ 2010 - 2011   San Luis Art Supply
- ➤ 1955 – 2005   Albert's Florist

Address 1118
- ➤ 2009 - 2011   Baxter Moerman Jewelry
- ➤ 1990   Albert's Florist
- ➤ 1985   Vacant
- ➤ 1970 – 1980   Rose and Henry Tailors
- ➤ 1965   Laura's Gifts
- ➤ 1960   Merle Norman Cosmetics
- ➤ 1945 – 1950   Liquor Store
- ➤ 1930 – 1935   Midland Counties Public Service
- ➤ 1925   Public Market

**1120
Morro**

1120 Morro Street * Demolished June 2011

- ➢ 2010 – 2011   San Luis Art Supply/Demolished
- ➢ 1985 – 2005   Rose and Henry Tailors
- ➢ 1975   Drapery Dan
- ➢ 1970   La Casa Wigs
- ➢ 1960 – 1965   Margo Larry Health Foods
- ➢ 1945 – 1955   Elite Beauty Salon

1126-1128-1130 Morro Street

Address 1126

- 2009 – 2011   Granada Bistro
- 2000 – 2009   Beary Cute Bears / Vacant / Retro
- 1995   That's Advertising
- 1985 – 1990   That's Video
- 1975   Hawk Humanist Imp.
- 1960 – 1970   Air Force Recurting
- 1955   Christian Science Reading Room
- 1945 – 1950   Liquor Store
- 1940   Christian Science Reading Room
- 1935   Barber

Address 1128

-
- 1030 – 2011   Granada Hotel/ Retrofitting, June 2011

Address 1130

- 2009 – 2011   Granada Bistro
- 2010 – 2011   Retrofitting   June 2011 Ground Floor/2nd Floor
- 1995 – 2005   Designer Watch Shop
- 1990   Gift Shop
- 1985   Country Junctions
- 1980   Hawks Humanist
- 1975   Moor Coffee
- 1960 – 1970   Conklin Insurance

1144
Morro

1144 Morro Street

➤ 2011 – 1995   Union Bank
➤ 1965 – 1990   Security Bank

From 1906 to 1960 the old Elk's Club occupied this corner of Morro and Marsh Streets.

Elks Theatre, San Luis Obispo, California.   S-604

Garden Street

1108 Garden

Garden Street was originally a dirt road that went from the mission to the mission gardens. In 1870, there was no Garden Street. At that time Garden Street was simply a dirt path that went to the gardens and vineyards where fruits and other produce were grown.

1108 Garden Street

➢ 2011 – 1950   Maino Building
The Maino building
was construced in 1903

The Maino family was and continues to be very important in the history of San Luis Obispo. The Maino Construction Company was started in 1881 by Joseph Maino who was born in Italy in 1850. Mr. Maino started his company the same year he arrived in San Luis Obispo. He learned the carpentry and building trade while in Italy and used these skills to start his business. He was responsible for building many buildings in San Luis Obispo, not only downtown, but many buildings at Cal Poly. Today the Maino family continues the family traditions, which would make their family founder very proud.

1119 Garden

1119 Garden Street
Built in 1912 by James Maino

- ➤ 1990 – 2011   SLO Brew (and a few other name variations)
- ➤ 1985   Granny's Store
- ➤ 1960 – 1980   **Hana's Farm Supply and Equipment**
- ➤ 1940 – 1955   Union Hardware
- ➤ 1926 – 1940   Hardware Store/Plumbing and Tin Shop
- ➤ 1912 – 1925   C. L. Johnson commercial building

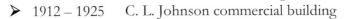

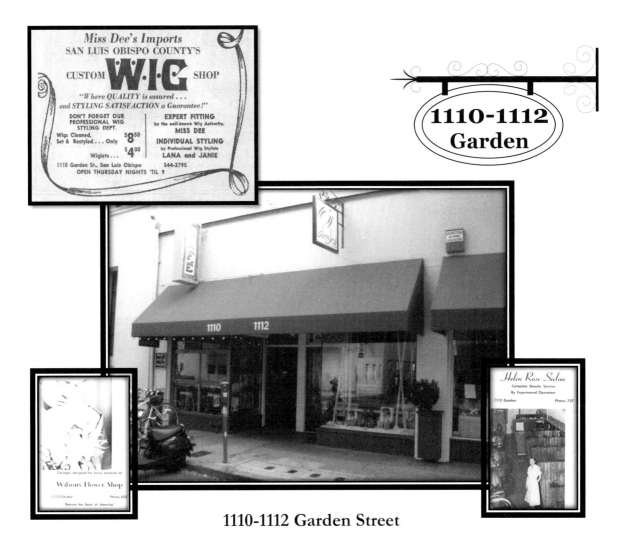

1110-1112 Garden

1110-1112 Garden Street

Address 1110
- ➤ 1985 – 2011   Linnea's Cafe
- ➤ 1969 – 1980   **Miss Dee Wigs**
- ➤ 1960   Elfrieda's Fashions
- ➤ 1940 -1955   **Wilson Florist**

Address 1112
- ➤ 2005 – 2011   Ahshe Day Spa
- ➤ 1990 – 2000   Mary North Beauty
- ➤ 1975 – 1985   Shalinar Beauty
- ➤ 1960 – 1970   Beauty Salon
- ➤ 1955   **Helen Rose Salon**
- ➤ 1940 – 1950   Ollie's Beauty Shop
- ➤ 1930   Motz Ladies Haberdasery

1114-1118 Garden

Many of our downtown buildings have names on them, and Garden Street is home to the "Barrett Block." A man named **Thomas Barrett** had a real estate and insurance business in 1904 at 1114 Garden. Thomas Barrett Sr. and Jr. were one of the first long standing real estate and insurance businesses in town and were active community members.

1114-1118 Garden Street

Address 1114	
➢ 1978 – 2011	Garden Street Goldsmiths
➢ 1955 – 1978	Optometrist
➢ 1940 – 1950	Doctor Offices
➢ 1935	Wilson Florist
➢ 1905 – 1920	**Thomas Barrett Insurance and Real Estate**

Address 1118	
➢ 2006 – 2011	Garden Street Goldsmiths
➢ 1981 – 2006	Hamilton Estate Jewrlery
➢ 1960 – 1980	Beltone Hearing Services
➢ 1950	San Luis Brokerage/Real Estate
➢ 1945	Real Estate

1123-1125 Garden

1125 - 1123 Garden Street

Address 1125
- ➤ 1985 -2011   Melody House
- ➤ 1965 – 1980   Melody House/ Alcoholics Anon
- ➤ 1960   Alcoholics Anon
- ➤ 1950   Adjustment Bureau
- ➤ 1930   Sewing Machine
- ➤ 1924 – 2011   Apartments

Address 1123
- ➤ 1960 – 2011   Christian Science Reading Room
- ➤ 1945 – 1955   Farm Credit Assoc.
- ➤ 1935   Farmers Insurance
- ➤ 1930   Preuss Press

This building was known as the Smith Building. This was a 40 ft. by 60 ft structure originally, and in 1924, a second story was added and construction was completed. Normally stores were below and apartments were above.

1127 Garden

1127 Garden Street

- 2010 -2011   Bel Fries
- 2005   Vacant
- 1995 – 2000   Anything Educational
- 1976 – 1990   T.W. Paper Clip
- 1970 – 1975   Dick's Office Machine
- 1960 – 1965   Dress Shop (Della)
- 1955   Guarantee Building and Loan
- 1930 – 1950   Building and Loan
- 1925   Sewing Machine Shop

Authorized Southern Pacific Watch Inspector

DON ANDREWS
Jeweler
LIBERTY 3-4543

1120 GARDEN St.   SAN LUIS OBISPO, CA.

1120-1124 Garden Street

Address 1120
- ➤ 2005 – 2011   Gene Francis Gallery
- ➤ 2000   Paper Planet
- ➤ 1990 – 1995   Nordic Imports
- ➤ 1970 – 1985   **Jewelry (Andrews)**
- ➤ 1950 – 1965   Real Estate

Address 1124
- ➤ 2000 – 2011   Finder's Keepers
- ➤ 1990   N'Chon gifts
- ➤ 1960 – 1985   Pete's Locksmith
- ➤ 1930 – 1950   Doctor's offices
- ➤ 1922   San Luis Dairy

1128 Garden

1128 Garden Street

    The building at 1128 Garden Street is the newest addition on the block. This building was built in 2002 and blends in with the rest of the block. There have been other businesses at this address in the past. Back in 1910, E E Long's Piano store was at this location before settling into his long-time business on Marsh Street.

    Back in the mission days, Garden Street was the footpath that went from the mission down Garden Street which led to the mission vineyards and gardens. The citizens began simply calling the path the garden path which progressed to becoming a frequently traveled street in downtown San Luis Obispo and over the years Garden Street became a part of the city.

2006 – 2011   Hamilton Estates Jewelry occupies 1128-A

1130 Garden

1130 Garden Street

- ➤ 2010 - 2011   Retrofitting 2011
- ➤ 2005   Jump Hair
- ➤ 2000   Attorney/Beauty Salon
- ➤ 1990 – 1995   Attorney/Underground Audio
- ➤ 1985   Attorney/Audio Ecstacy
- ➤ 1970 – 1975   Insurance/Multi. Businesses
- ➤ 1960 – 1965   Coast Counties Adjust Bureau
- ➤ 1955   American Cancer Society
- ➤ 1930 – 1950   Doctor's offices

1129 Garden

Today, in 2011, there seems to be three businesses with the address 1129, but it was not always so confusing. The picture to the right is the original 1129 and next door was 1131 and then 1135. These three businesses were constructed in 1883 and moved to this location in 1897. Before people had to worry about plumbing and electricity, a building was basically a large box that could be moved around. These buildings will go under major construction in the near future, along with the majority of Garden Street. Cherish these wonderful memories of Garden Street.

1129 Garden Street

- ➤ 2011   Aurignac Realty
- ➤ 2010   Furnishing
- ➤ 2005   Secret Garden
- ➤ 1995 – 2000   Casa Blanc Travel
- ➤ 1985 – 1990   Up The Wall Wallpaper
- ➤ 1960 – 1980   Noble Sewing Service
- ➤ 1950   Strader's Lock
- ➤ 1935   Barber shop
- ➤ 1905   Millinery

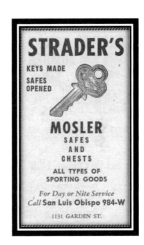

1129 Garden Street (also known as 1131)

- ➤ 2011   Clothing/Vacant May 2011
- ➤ 2005 – 2010   Clothes
- ➤ 1995 – 2000   Casa Blanc Travel
- ➤ 1985 – 1990   Up The Wall Wallpaper
- ➤ 1960 – 1980   Noble Sewing Service
- ➤ 1960 – 1965   Dick's Machines
- ➤ 1945 – 1950   Locksmith
- ➤ 1935 – 1950   **Strader's Locksmith**

1129 Garden Street (also known as 1135)

- ➤ 2005 - 2011   Lil Lil Clever
- ➤ 1995 – 2000   Casa Blanc Travel
- ➤ 1985 – 1990   Up The Wall Wallpaper
- ➤ 1960 – 1980   Noble Sewing Service

Over the years all three of these addresses were at times occupied by a single business or by multiple businesses. As ownership changed hands so did addresses.

1137
Garden

1137 Garden Street

- ➢ 2005 – 2011   California Blonde
- ➢ 1996 – 2000   Gardener's Cottage
- ➢ 1990   LMT Apparel
- ➢ 1975 – 1985   New Dawn Clothes
- ➢ 1960 – 1970   Covell Shoe Repair
- ➢ 1940 – 1950   The Wardrobe
- ➢ 1930 – 1935   San Luis Matteress
- ➢ 1910 – 1915   Sewing Machine

Board of Trade
San Luis Obispo
1903

Andrews Banking Co.
SAN LUIS OBISPO, CAL.

Mrs Earle E. Hughes
No 1111 S. St.
Fresno
Cal.

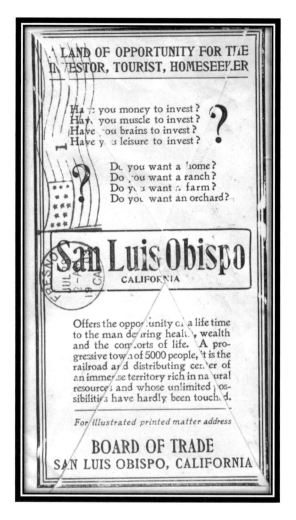

A LAND OF OPPORTUNITY FOR THE
INVESTOR, TOURIST, HOMESEEKER

Have you money to invest?
Have you muscle to invest?
Have you brains to invest?
Have you leisure to invest?

Do you want a home?
Do you want a ranch?
Do you want a farm?
Do you want an orchard?

San Luis Obispo
CALIFORNIA

Offers the opportunity of a life time
to the man desiring health, wealth
and the comforts of life. A pro-
gressive town of 5000 people, it is the
railroad and distributing center of
an immense territory rich in natural
resources and whose unlimited pos-
sibilities have hardly been touched.

For illustrated printed matter address

BOARD OF TRADE
SAN LUIS OBISPO, CALIFORNIA

The Chamber of Commerce is always an important organization for promoting a city.
Bringing as many tourists to the city is important to bring dollars to the city and businesses. In
San Luis Obispo, the Chamber of Commerce was known in 1903 as the Board of Trade. The
Board of Trade for San Luis Obispo would send out thousands of these types of promotions.

San Luis Obispo, California
**A LAND OF OPPORTUNITY FOR THE
INVESTOR, TOURIST, HOMESEEKER**
Board of Trade, 1903

Broad Street

1010
Broad

I honestly have no idea of how or why Broad Street acquired its name. I know lots of cities have a Broad or Broadway Street. That's my best guess. If someone else knows, please share your information with me. I do know this though: In 1870, Broad Street was an original street in town. Broad Street started at Stenner Creek near Walnut Street and followed the same direction as it does today.

1010 - 1020 Broad Street

Address 1010
- ➤ 1970 – 2011   San Luis Obispo Museum of Art
- ➤ 1960 – 1965   Chiropractor (Otto)

Address 1020
- ➤ 1965   Arts Tailor
- ➤ 1960   State Department of Agriculture
- ➤ 1955   McNamera Realty
- ➤ 1940 – 1950   Lawerence Realty

1019-1021 Broad

Stop By And See A Demonstration At The
San Luis Telephone Gallery

We carry a complete selection of
accessories to enhance your telephone

1023 Broad St...San Luis Obispo   541-6575

1023, 1021 and 1019 Broad Street

Address 1023		Address 1021		Address 1019	
➤ 2011	Bambu Batu	➤1990 - 2011	Old World Rug	➤ 2005 – 2011	Antique Boutique
➤ 1980 – 2000	**Telephone Gallery**	➤1985	Sofa Shop	➤ 1985 – 2000	The Framery
➤ 1960 – 1970	B & B Antiques	➤1980	House of Candle	➤ 1955 – 1970	Beno's
➤ 1930 - 1937	Miller Plumbing and Heating. This business took the entire building	➤1975	B & B Antiques		
		➤1960 – 1970	Your and My Furniture		

1040
Broad

1040 Broad Street

- ➢ 2010 – 2011   Creekside Brewing
- ➢ 2005   Grappolo's
- ➢ 2000   Vacant
- ➢ 1990 – 1995   Rythym Café
- ➢ 1985   Bakery Café
- ➢ 1980   Silver Lining Fabrics
- ➢ 1975   Mission Antiques
- ➢ 1965 – 1970   Gamboni's Antiques
- ➢ 1960   Thrift Store

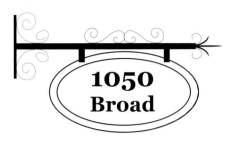

1050 Broad Street

- ➤ 2010 – 2011   Shift Beauty Shop
- ➤ 2005   TKD Surf Shop
- ➤ 1995   Body Suite
- ➤ 1990   Gary Paul clothes
- ➤ 1985   Vacant
- ➤ 1980   Devine Decadence

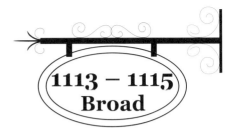

1113 – 1115 Broad

1113-1115 Broad Street

- ➤ 2010 – 2011   Hemp Shack
- ➤ 1985 – 1990   Mr. C's Chicken Natural
- ➤ 1965 – 1980   Don's Shoes/Adam Antiques
- ➤ 1960   Weddell's Used Furniture
- ➤ 1950   Walker's Used Furniture
- ➤ 1940   Oliver Street

1113 Broad Street is apartments on the second floor.

1121
Broad

1121 Broad Street

- ➤ 1994 – 2011   Big Sky Cafe
- ➤ 1990   Dr. West Indies bar
- ➤ 1985   Tom Buckle's Keyboards
- ➤ 1965 – 1980   Idler's Appliances
- ➤ 1955 – 1965   Reed's Paint and Wallpaper
- ➤ 1930 – 1940   Used furniture
- ➤ 1905 – 1915   Blacksmith shop

Here is a business that was on Morro Street for over 25 years. From 1961 to 1985, Farley's was a family favorite and a great place to get some tasty desserts or your favorite burger.

Farley's
A Family
Favorite

farley's family
RESTAURANTS

YOUR HOME GOODNESS PLACE, HOMEMADE PIES & DESSERTS

SAN LUIS OBISPO: 1135 Morro St. (Downtown San Luis)
ARROYO GRANDE: 611 Grand Ave. (Just off the Freeway)

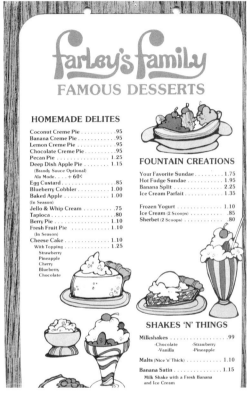

farley's family
FAMOUS DESSERTS

HOMEMADE DELITES

Coconut Creme Pie	.95
Banana Creme Pie	.95
Lemon Creme Pie	.95
Chocolate Creme Pie	.95
Pecan Pie	1.25
Deep Dish Apple Pie	1.15
(Brandy Sauce Optional)	
Ala Mode	+60¢
Egg Custard	.85
Blueberry Cobbler	1.00
Baked Apple	1.00
(In Season)	
Jello & Whip Cream	.75
Tapioca	.80
Berry Pie	1.10
Fresh Fruit Pie	1.10
(In Season)	
Cheese Cake	1.10
With Topping	1.25
Strawberry	
Pineapple	
Cherry	
Blueberry	
Chocolate	

FOUNTAIN CREATIONS

Your Favorite Sundae	1.75
Hot Fudge Sundae	1.95
Banana Split	2.25
Ice Cream Parfait	1.35
Frozen Yogurt	1.10
Ice Cream (2 Scoops)	.85
Sherbet (2 Scoops)	.80

SHAKES 'N' THINGS

Milkshakes	.99
-Chocolate -Strawberry	
-Vanilla -Pineapple	
Malts (Nice 'n' Thick)	1.10
Banana Satin	1.15
Milk Shake with a Fresh Banana and Ice Cream	

FARLEYS FAMILY PRESENTS

INTERNATIONAL BURGER BAR

Char-broiled and served with lettuce, tomato and pickles

1. THE OL' FASHION	2.25	8. MUSHROOM PROVENCIAL	2.60
2. THE ALPINE	2.40	9. TEXAS CHILE BURGER	2.60
3. THE RUSSIAN	2.50	10. CISCO PISTOL	2.60
4. THE GERMAN	2.60	11. HULA BURGER	2.60
5. ITALIANO	2.60	12. THE BRITISHER	3.15
6. ORTEGA PEPPER & CHEESE	2.60	13. THE BONANZA	3.20
7. CATTLEMEN'S PRIDE	2.75	14. THE CALIFORNIAN	3.25
		15. THE LUMBER JACK	3.50

OTHER HOUSE SPECIALTIES

SALADS & CHILI DISHES

*Served with hot sourdough bread, french garlic bread,
Hot Corn Bread, or Rye Krisp or crackers*

FIESTA SALAD	3.25	CHILI & CORNBREAD	1.20
CHEF'S SALAD	3.50	CHILI SIZE	3.75
		TUNA (or TURKEY SALAD en BOUQUET)	2.95
FRUIT SALAD	3.50	FRESH SPINACH SALAD	2.25
HALF CHEF or FRUIT	2.95		

1127-1127A Broad

1127 – 1127A Broad Street

Address 1127

- 2011   Broad Street Tavern (June 2011)
- 2010   Vacant/retrofit
- 2005 – 1985   Boston Bagel
- 1980   House of Lamp Shades
- 1930 – 1975   Yours and My Furniture
-
-

Address 1127A

- 2011   Tropical Chocolate
- 2000 – 2005   Luna Rustica
- 1995   Plum's children
- 1990   Pacific furniture
- 1985   Phoenix books
- 1980   House of Lamps
- 1930 – 1975   Yours and My Furniture

1131 Broad Street

➢ 2011   Wild Donkey Café
➢ 1995 – 2005   Tio Alberto's
➢ 1990   Mission Inport clothes
➢ 1980 – 1985   **Dick's Office Machine**
➢ 1975   Toby's Restaurant
➢ 1970   Grandma's Pancakes
➢ 1965   Edna's Country Restaurant
➢ 1960   Hickenbottom Hair
➢ 1955   Capri
➢ 1950   Salvation Army
➢ 1935 – 1940   Melin's Market

1108 Broad Street

- ➤ 2010 – 2011   An Apple A Day as of August 2011/Giordano's Fruit Freeze
- ➤ 2010   Nor Jewelry
- ➤ 1990 – 2005   **Blazing Blenders**
- ➤ 1985   Vacant
- ➤ 1975 – 1980   Aaron Insurance

1228-1234
Broad

1228 and 1234 Broad

Address 1228

> 2000 - 2011   Changes Beauty

> 1975 – 1995   Jason's Hair House

> 1955 – 1970   Kamm Realty

Address 1234

> 2010 – 2011   Furniture Store
> 1990 – 2005   **Villa Auto Repair**
> 1965 – 1985   Auto Clinic Repair
> 1960   Studebaker and Packard
>   Auto/garage
> 1950   Green's Auto
> 1940- 1950   Bello's Auto

1301
Broad

1301 Broad Street

- ➤ 1998 – 2011   A & R Furniture closes in Summer of 2011
- ➤ 1970 – 1990   Nearly New Furniture/Reis Furniture
- ➤ 1961 – 1965   Weatherby's Furniture
- ➤ 1950 – 1955   White's Furniture
- ➤ 1930 – 1940   Union Feed and Seed
- ➤ 1905 – 1920   Modern Steam Laundry   The Modern Steam Laundry was pre-1905 as well.

1301 was a shared address with more than two different businesses within the building. The above businesses were the main businesses during their time.

Nipomo Street

991
Nipomo

991 Nipomo Street

➤ 1971 – 2011   Reis Family Mortuary & Crematory
➤ 1935 – 1970   Harmony Valley Creamery/Challenge

Harmony Valley Creamery

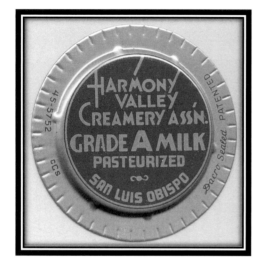

The Harmony Valley Creamery had a very long history in San Luis Obispo. Home delivery of milk in glass milk bottles was one of the perks of the past. Challenge butter also became a product of the Harmony Valley Creamery in later years.

KEEPING IN TOUCH WITH THE PAST--Mortician Gene Reis with some of the items in his San Luis Obispo, Calif. mortuary museum. (PHOTO CREDIT: John Malmin, Los Angeles Times) Illustrates story slugged MORTUARY MUSEUM by Charles Hillinger (Times) to move over wire on Monday, Dec. 22, 1975.

LOS ANGELES TIMES / WASHINGTON POST NEWS SERVICE

Times Mirror Square / Los Angeles, California 90053 / Telephone (213) 625-2345

This was a newspaper article I purchased over the internet. It is dated January 4 1976 from the Los Angeles Times news service. The article talks about the museum Gene Reis has in the basement of the mortuary. Several years ago Mr. Reis was nice enough to take me on a tour of his basement and it is indeed full of wonderful things from the past. He gave me the Challenge butter box on page 90, which I have always treasured.

This is a token that was given to people after the depression was declared over by Reilly One Stop Service, a department store, to encourage shoppers to start shopping again.

The Green Bus token was purchased by people who would ride on the Green Bus Service to pay their fare. The bus company was on Archer Street and the busses ran all over town.

This souvenir token from 1914 is something I purchased online. I'm not sure what event this commemorated, but the beehive on the bottom must be a clue.

1023 Nipomo Street

- ➤ 2010 - 2011   Nordic Mart yarn supplies
- ➤ 1970 – 2000   Vacant/storage
- ➤ 1945   McBride Sheet Metal Works
- ➤ 1920   Crown Soda Works
- ➤ 1915   Bottling Company

This is an actual bottle from the Crown Soda Works factory. The center of the bottle reads **Soda Works** and above that the bottle reads **San Luis Obispo.** The bottom part of the circle reads **L. Albert. Prop.**

1010 Nipomo

1010 Nipomo Street

- ➤ 1995 – 2011   Children's Museum
- ➤ 1985 – 1990   Vacant
- ➤ 1970 – 1980   Transmission Shop
- ➤ 1965   Phil's Machine Shop
- ➤ 1960   Paul's Garage

1024 Nipomo Street

- ➢ 2010 – 2011   Tonitas Mexican Food
- ➢ 1990 - 2005   Burrito Wagon
- ➢ 1975 – 1985   Larry's Glamour
- ➢ 1965 – 1970   Mirianm's Beauty Shop
- ➢ 1950 – 1960   Beauty Shop

This is a small sterling silver spoon with Mission San Luis Obispo on it and the back is dated Oct. 22, 1905. This is a sample of things I have bought over the years using the internet. I bought this from someone in Topeka, Kansas.

**1051
Nipomo**

1051 Nipomo Street

This building is part of the Creamery complex near the corner of Higuera and Nipomo Streets in downtown SLO. The Creamery was named for the Golden State Creamery that was located here for many decades. Golden State provided bottled milk to towns all over California from the early 1920's to the 1950's when it changed its name from Golden State to Foremost Dairies. The building above has been several businesses since the creamery closed in the 1970's. The most memorable business at this address was Tortilla Flats Mexican Restaurant which was located here from 1975 to 2005. In 2007, Don's Karaoke Bar opened but closed in January 2008. Ciopinot's restaurant, which opened in 2009, is the current keeper of one of most historic buildings in downtown San Luis Obispo.

Palm Street

751
Palm

751 Palm Street

Mission College Preparatory High School was dedicated on August 19, 1926. Mission College Prep (MCP) is a private school which charges tuition to attend, so I would consider MCP a successful business in our community. You can see that MCP has kept its architectural beauty over the years when you compare the current top picture with the bottom picture from the 1920's.

798 Palm

Richard Chong in his candy store, which he started in 1950 and was open until his death in 1978.

798 Palm Street
Built in 1925 by Addison Chong

- ➤ 2000 – 2011   Real Estate businesses
- ➤ 1985 – 1990   Flynn's Ladies clothes
- ➤ 1980   Archimedia Architectural
- ➤ 1950 – 1978   **Chong's Candy Shop**
- ➤ 1925 – 1950   Chong's Chow Mein Restaurant

Thanks to The Tribune/Larry Jamison for the use of Mr. Chong's picture.

San Luis Obispo, Chinatown

Ah Louis was the leader in the Chinese community during the late 1800's in San Luis Obispo's Chinatown. Many considered Ah Louis the unofficial mayor of Chinatown. Ah Louis had a food and dry goods store which also acted as a post office, bank, employment agency, and other various services that Ah Louis provided. There were several other types of businesses in Chinatown along this block of Palm Street. Those businesses included restaurants, a joss house, boarding houses, gambling rooms, grocery, laundromats, and other types of businesses. Over the years this block of Palm Street became unpopular and many of the wooden buildings began to deteriorate. Most needed to be demolished in the 1950's. Today a parking structure occupies the block where once stood many old wooden buildings and Chinese businesses.

800
Palm

800 Palm Street (Built in 1886)

The Ah Louis store is the last building from the 1800's that reminds us of the Chinatown that was once an important part of the San Luis Obispo community. I was fortunate enough to know Howard Louis and interviewed him on two occasions. Howard was the son of Ah Louis and Howard and his wife ran the store for years and years. I remember bringing my daughters into the store and Mrs. Louis would remind my daughters not to touch anything in the store and to be careful. Howard had many classic Chinese toys, clothes, and an assortment of other items that someone would find in any Chinatown shop in Los Angeles or San Francisco. In addition to items for sale, he also had many wonderful stories about the history of Chinatown in SLO. In 2011, Vintage etc. occupy this address.

> San Luis Obispo
> July 7th 1885
>
> Proposal for mason
> work on Ah Louis
> Building
> For laying Brick
> Plastering and Cementing
> with Brick, Lime & Sand
> Cement and Scaffolding
> furnished on the ground
> Four Hundred and fifty
> dollars ($ 450)
>
> Fred Buh____
>
> (BRICKS TO BE SUPPLIED BY AH LOUIS BRICK YARD)

A Gift from Howard Louis

On one of my visits to interview Howard, he began showing me one picture after another with great stories that went with each picture. Many of the pictures had mold on them due to a leak in the roof. He pulled out a copy of the original contract for the "new" brick building that was built in 1886. I felt very honored that he took the time to show me so many of his documents and pictures, and that he gave me a copy of the above contract. I miss Howard and the great stories he would tell.

**811
Palm**

811 Palm Street

- ➤ 2011   Abraxas Energy
- ➤ 2005   Tetra Tech Enviroment
- ➤ 2000   Visual Systems
- ➤ 1955 – 1990   Carpenter's Union , Bartenders Union

815 Palm

815 Palm Street

➢   1950 – 2000   Mee Heng Low Chop Suey

Chinatown in San Luis Obispo has many great stories. The even numbered side of the street was the Wong family's (Ah Louis's real last name was Wong) side of Chinatown and the odd numbered side was the Ginn family's side of the street. I was once told that the Wong and the Ginn families would have disagreements and at times gun shots would be heard. This is one reason that the Ah Louis store had iron shutters on all of its windows. True or not, I always love to hear wild stories of San Luis Obispo.

817 Palm Street

The Palm Theater is one of the few businesses in the country that relies on solar power to produce the electricity it needs to operate. The solar panels are installed out of sight on the roof.

- ➤ 1990 – 2011   Palm Theater
- ➤ 1980 – 1985   Vacant
- ➤ 1955 – 1975   Employment Department

895,865,863,861
Palm

895-865-863-861 Palm Street

Addresses 863 – 865 – 895		Address 861	
➤ 1960 – 1971	Lucksinger Motors	➤ 2005 – 2011	Vacant
➤ 1949	Serafin's Paint	➤ 2000	Palindrones
➤		➤ 1995	Wild Billy Wongs
➤		➤ 1955 – 1985	Shanghai Low

    The 800 block of Palm Street was the heart of Chinatown in San Luis Obispo. Although much of this block is now parking lots, at one time this block was teeming with shops, restaurants, homes, boarding houses, auto sales, and other businesses of interest on both sides of the street. The future of this area of town will once again be teeming with shops, a hotel, and a variety of other businesses if a project known as the "Chinatown Project" starts constructions. In 2011 plans are still in motion.

Other Streets

280
Pismo

280 Pismo Street

The old San Luis Gas and Electric Company that still stands, since 1902, is one of my favorite buildings in town and was once a very important business. The very unique stone building is hidden away *near* the end of Pismo Street. This business supplied gas and electricity to the town and brought San Luis Obispo into the modern age by lighting the downtown streets so people could shop longer and feel safe while out after dark.

301 or 1901 Santa Barbara Street

Del Monte Café has been a part of our community since the turn of the century. The Robbins family started their grocery store in the early 1900's at this location when the address was 301 Santa Barbara Street. It was a grocery store for over 50 years until family members died and the building was condemned and boarded up. In 1981 the Del Monte once again became a business as a café in the neighborhood.

228 or 1880 Santa Barbara Street

Railroad Square was built at the turn of the Century as a warehouse for groceries which would then be distributed to the local markets in town. Channel Commercial Co. was the first business at this location and they must have been one of the first businesses to get a telephone because their telephone number was 93. The address was 228 at that time. Groceries were delivered by railroad cars and they had their own tracks behind the building for easy delivery. In 2011, the building has become a multi-use business location.

1638 Osos Street

- ➢ 1970 – Present **Gus's Grocery**
- ➢ 1955 – 1967 Thompson's Store
- ➢ 1930 Welch Brothers Store

350 High (Once 420 High)

The address here changed in the early 1970's. Here are some of the businesses that have occupied this building.

- ➢ 1985 – 2011 **High Street Deli**
- ➢ 1980 Vacant
- ➢ 1970 – 1975 Tiny's
- ➢ 1965 Silva Market
- ➢ 1960 Joaquin's Grocery
- ➢ 1934 Burton's Cash Store
- ➢ 1930 Page's Cash Store

1901 Broad Street

This little red brick building was a grocery store in the 1930's and then became Personality Beauty Shop in the 60's and 70's. The little brick business then became a barber shop in the 1970's and the 1980's. Today, the historical brick building is home to "The Giant Grinder Shop," a local favorite sandwich shop.

2145 Broad Street

➢ 1955 – Present   Manuel's Liquors
➢ Pre-1955   Manuel's Bar and
                          Steak House

Still Popular Businesses

1401 Osos Street

These were some of the businesses at 1401 Osos:

➢ 2011   Sidewalk Market
➢ 1985   Circle K Store
➢ 1975 – 1980   Kwik Way Store
➢ 1946 – 1970   New Park Grocery
➢ 1935   Cozy Corner
                Grocery
➢ 1930   Bell Grocery

214 Higuera Street

Paul's Cleaners has been one of the most successful long-standing businesses in San Luis Obispo. Paul's began business in 1952 and at one time they even had a second store downtown on Osos Street which closed around 1965.

Historical
Train Station
District

1011 Railroad Avenue
San Luis Obispo Train Station

The original depot was built in 1895 and was demolished in 1971. The current depot was built in 1942 and is one of the oldest businesses in San Luis Obispo.

1815 Osos Street
Hotel Park Building

The building at 1815 Osos was built in 1906 as a three-story boarding house. The building housed mostly railroad employees until the 1950's. The building was once the Axtell Hotel in the 20's and 30's, and in 1938 it was known as the Hotel Park. It now has 21 apartments upstairs and various businesses on the ground floor.

Corner of Morro and Monterey Street, circa 1910

    This is one of my favorite photos that I have bought over the years from people across the country. This is a picture of what the corner of Morro and Monterey Street looked like before the Anderson Hotel was built on this location. The two men in the picture are Erwin Kaiser and Harry Albert. There was a bowling alley and a billiards hall at this location. You can easily read the "Mallery's Pop Corn Crisperets" sign. I'm not sure what a pop corn crisperet was, but it must have been a snack at the turn of the century. The advertisement on the middle building reads OBAK which was a "mouthpiece cigarette" which is written under OBAK on the sign. The Anderson Hotel was completed in 1923, so this picture is a rare look at stores that were there before the city landmark hotel was built. I'm glad I got to share this photo with my readers.

**520
Dana**

520 Dana Street
Independent Order of Odd Fellows (IOOF)

The Independent Order of Odd Fellows (IOOF), Chorro Lodge, was established March 3, 1870. The founding members were all community leaders, who included Mr. Pepperman, Mr. Spooner, Mr. DeWitt, Mr. Johnson, and several other movers and shakers of town. Over the years the Chorro Lodge moved to several locations. Their first meeting hall was in an old adobe, then they moved to a building on Higuera, then to Marsh Street, and next to Monterey Street lodgings. Finally in 1942 the current location on Dana Street was purchased and on July 6, 1942, the first meeting was held and a formal dedication was celebrated on Saturday, Sept. 19, 1942. Dancing, dinner, and refreshments were all part of the dedication ceremony. Today the I.O.O.F. continues to be an important part of our community with a growing membership.

Exposition Park Race Track

One of the businesses in town during the 1920's was auto racing. San Luis Obispo had its own auto racing track called Exposition Park, which was near South Street between Broad and Higuera Streets. Today there are houses which cover up all remnants of the old race track. What a lot of people aren't aware of is that Universal Pictures shot a silent movie in 1924 called _Sporting Youth_ starring Reginald Denny. Much of the movie was shot in Monterey, California, but the race track scenes were shot in San Luis Obispo at our own Exposition Park race track, which was known back in those days as the "fastest one-mile dirt track in California". The poster on this page is the poster used to promote the movie. Unfortunately, I have never been able to find a copy of this silent movie, which would be a great part of the history of the city.

Sleep Off the Hi-Way Motel

145
South

This is the Sleep Off the Hi-Way Motel during the 1960's. The motel goes back to at least the 1940's. The address is 145 South Street but during the 1940's the address was 1000 South Street. The motel had 34 small rooms for rent by the day, week or month. For one person it was $65 a month or $90 for two people per month.

The picture to the right is what the motel looks like today. To my surprise the complex looks very much the same as it did 70 years ago. The office is still there and the small rooms are still there just as both pictures show. I would guess that this motel is one of the oldest in town. I have driven by this complex hundreds of times and never would have guessed that it had such a rich history in our town.

Brooks Woodcraft

2087 Santa Barbara Street

This family-owned business has been part of the San Luis Obispo community since 1964. In 1965 their address was 517, but as frequently happens, the city decided to change the address of the entire block. The family has been selling unfinished furniture since the beginning and today has included selling antiques. It is amazing to have a family-owned business for over 47 at the same location. Congratulations.

AUGUST 14 & 15, 1965

8th ANNUAL RUNNING
SAN LUIS OBISPO COUNTY AIRPORT
ROAD RACES

Sponsored by San Luis Obispo Junior Chamber of Commerce

With cooperation of | El Camino Foreign Car Club
California Sports Car Club Region
Sports Car Club of America
Long Beach MG Car Club

This pass must be worn at all times.
NOT TRANSFERABLE
The use of this pass is revocable and is confined to individuals over 21 years of age.
PRESS

GLOBE TICKET CO., L.A. 495

000243

Road Races, 1965

Way back in 1965, the county airport was used for road races. San Luis Obispo has always been a city which welcomed racing. Back in the 1920's we had Exposition Park, as you have already read, and starting in the 1950's we sponsored road racing. This press pass was used by the local newspaper to report all the fast cars that participated in this annual event.

1708 Beach Street
Sandercock Moving and Storage
In business since 1872

1708 Beach

1708 Beach Street

     Sandercock Moving and Storage has been at this location since the late 1940's, but the company has been around since 1872. According to the Sandercock web site, the company is the oldest family owned business in San Luis Obispo County. The business had its first location at 856 Higuera Street until the mid 1930's. The company at one time had over 300 horses and mules used in the moving of just about anything.

     By 1950, the Sandercock Company was enjoying their new location and the family continued to run the company. The company was started by William Sandercock in 1872 and then he turned over the reins to his son Norman. By the late 1920's, the company was fully motorized and one of their most famous customers was William R. Hearst. Today the Sandercock family still enjoys the pleasure of running the oldest family-run business in the county.

Very Lower Higuera, circa 1930's

      This photo is an incredible view of the road you would drive up the coast of California to come into the wonderful town of San Luis Obispo from the south. At one time Higuera Street was Highway 101 through San Luis Obispo. You need to get out a magnifying glass to look at the cool sign you would drive under that reads "San Luis Obispo" as you would enter the town. You can also read a sign that says "Aut-O-Tel" which was the Beechwood Hotel at 74 Higuera Street during the 1930's. You can also read a sign that says "15 cents a gallon for gas." The Aut-O-Tel is the complex to the right edge of the photo. The larger buildings were probably city-owned warehouses for city vehicles. This is truly a wonderful look back into the history of San Luis Obispo.

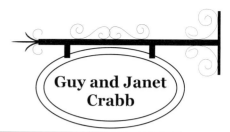

Guy and Janet Crabb
Standing next to their 1957 Chevy truck in front of County Historical Museum.

This is the last book on the streets of San Luis Obispo. Writing these three history books of downtown San Luis Obispo has been an incredible experience. One of the greatest parts about writing these books has been talking to the people who have lived in town for many years and were willing to share their memories. Another great thing about writing these books has been the people who have thanked me for documenting some important history of our town. As San Luis Obispo continues to change in the years to come, I hope my three books will let people remember the past and celebrate the future. Thanks!

Coming soon from Guy Crabb Publishing

San Luis Obispo
100 Years of Downtown Businesses
Updated Higuera Street

Beach Towns
100 Years of Downtown Businesses
Morro Bay & Pismo Beach

~ Also ~

Matted enlargements of many of the pictures in all
three books. Send an email and request a brochure
for the picture selections and prices.

Ours readers are our most important resource, and we value your input, suggestions, and ideas. We would also appreciate any old photos of businesses or street scenes from around town.

To order additional copies and/or to contact us, please mail or email us at:

Guy Crabb Publishing
P.O. Box 994
San Luis Obispo, Ca 93405
crabbx5@charter.net
www.slo100years.com